SpringerBriefs in Information Systems

Series Editor
Jörg Becker

More information about this series at http://www.springer.com/series/10189

Georg Hodosi • Lazar Rusu

Risks, Relationships and Success Factors in IT Outsourcing

A Study in Large Companies

 Springer

Georg Hodosi
Computer and Systems Sciences
Stockholm University
Stockholm, Sweden

Lazar Rusu
Computer and Systems Sciences
Stockholm University
Stockholm, Sweden

ISSN 2192-4929   ISSN 2192-4937   (electronic)
SpringerBriefs in Information Systems
ISBN 978-3-030-05924-8   ISBN 978-3-030-05925-5   (eBook)
https://doi.org/10.1007/978-3-030-05925-5

Library of Congress Control Number: 2018965607

This Springer imprint is published by the registered company Springer Nature Switzerland AG
The registered company address is: Gewerbestrasse 11, 6330 Cham, Switzerland

Preface

This book is an extract from Georg Hodosi's dissertation for the Degree of Doctor of Philosophy in Computer and Systems Sciences at Stockholm University, Sweden, defended on 15 June 2017. The title of the dissertation is "Information Technology Outsourcing in Large Companies in Sweden: A Perspective on Risks, Relationships and Success Factors".

The research in this book investigates large private companies in Sweden that have outsourced their information technology (IT). A considerable proportion of IT outsourcing (ITO) is unsuccessful. For IT service buyers, this could cause that IT does not fully work, entailing problems with the network, application, infrastructure and security, with serious consequences such as a loss of customers' confidence and significantly increased costs. Therefore, the main research goal was to analyse and define ways to improve ITO for the buyer organizations. This main research goal was accomplished through three research goals: (1) to develop a method for risk assessment in IT outsourcing, (2) to identify the important factors in IT outsourcing relationship and (3) to identify the success factors in IT outsourcing.

A study was also performed to explore IT decision makers' acceptance of the developed method and their use of it for assessing the ITO risks. The second research goal investigated how to improve service buyers' ITO relationship with their providers. A well-working ITO relationship is a critical determinant of successful ITO and is relevant to the whole ITO life cycle. This research goal was achieved by identifying and analysing the most important factors in ITO relationships, including a prioritized list of those factors that are highly recommended for use in creating and maintaining a good ITO relationship.

The third research goal examined how to improve ITO by identifying and prioritizing the success factors in ITO. This research has identified the ITO success factors in large companies and provided a prioritized list of them to be applied in these companies with a description of the value that they could create from their implementation during the ITO life cycle. Moreover, the success factors identified in large companies were compared with those identified in medium-sized companies, which could give an indication to the researchers in this field that company size matters in regard to the implementation order of the identified success factors.

Stockholm, Sweden   Georg Hodosi
Stockholm, Sweden   Lazar Rusu

Contents

About the Authors

Georg Hodosi Ph.D., is an affiliate researcher at the Department of Computer and Systems Sciences, Stockholm University, Sweden. He has a Ph.D. and a Ph.Lic. in computer and systems sciences from Stockholm University, an M.Sc. in engineering from Lund University and an M.Sc. in education in technology and mathematics from Stockholm Institute of Education. He has more than 25 years of professional experience in companies like Ericsson in Sweden and Mannesmann in Germany in different areas such as strategic sourcing, project management, quality assurance, line management and software development. His research interest is in IT outsourcing, and he has about 15 years' experience within outsourcing and insourcing.

He can be contacted by email: hodosi@dsv.su.se.

Lazar Rusu Ph.D., is Professor at the Department of Computer and Systems Sciences, Stockholm University, Sweden. He is involved in teaching and research in IT management and has a professional experience of over 30 years both industrial and academic in the information systems area. His research interest is mainly in IT governance, business-IT alignment and IT outsourcing. The results of his research have been published in proceedings of top international conferences like ECIS, HICSS, AMCIS, PACIS and ISD and journals like *Computers in Human Behavior*, *Industrial Management & Data Systems*, *Information Systems Management*, *Journal of Global Information Technology Management* and *Journal of Information Technology Theory and Applications*, among others. He is an author of a number of book chapters and co-editor of the following books published by Springer: *Information Technology Governance in Public Organizations: Theory and Practice*, 2017, and *Information Systems, E-Learning, and Knowledge Management Research, Communications in Computer and Information Science*, vol. 278, 2012.

He can be contacted by email: lrusu@dsv.su.se.

List of Figures

Chapter 1
IT Outsourcing: Definition, Importance, Trends and Research

Abstract This chapter presents the definition of Information Technology Outsourcing (ITO), the importance and trends in ITO, the research problem, goals, and motivations including the delimitations of performing research in ITO in large companies.

Keywords Information Technology · IT outsourcing · IT outsourcing risks · IT outsourcing relationships · IT outsourcing success factors · Large companies

1.1 IT Outsourcing: Definition, Importance and Trends

Outsourcing is an inter-organizational activity between buying organizations, also called service buyer organizations (abbreviated to service buyers) and one or several seller organizations, also referred to as providers, vendors or suppliers. Usually we have used the terms service buyer, service provider and IT services in this book.

In ITO research and the ITO industry, there are many definitions of ITO. Below, we refer to Leimeister (2010), who describes 25 definitions of information technology outsourcing suggested by different researchers. Leimeister (2010, pp. 20–21) proposes the following definition: "handing over to one or more third party vendors (i.e., legally independent) the provision of some or all of an organization's IS functions such as, e.g., IT assets, activities, people, processes, or services for a contractually agreed monetary fee and period of time". We adopt this definition. It highlights that outsourcing is a contractual agreement including interrelated and ongoing exchanges and responsibilities. One of the most frequent uses of IT service delivery is running and maintaining the service buyer's IT infrastructure. Another important function is the maintenance, help and support of IT applications provided for the buying organization. We also want to mention that we do not count the hiring of contract workers as ITO. If a temporary worker or contractor worker is under the supervision of the IT organization, we see it as a staff augmentation. The definition of ITO that we intend to employ is the movement of work done in-house to a service provider that performs and manages the work. The service provider takes on the responsibility for achieving the contracted results (Computer Economics Inc. 2017).

The dispersion of the ITO market, according to Leimeister (2010) it is attributed to two main circumstances. Firstly, the interest in ITO is a consequence of a shift in business strategy. For this purpose, company managers consider ITO as a strategy to concentrate on core competencies and improve companies' competitive edge. Secondly, the interest in ITO is due to the lack of clarity about the value that IT delivers. According to Leimeister (2010), many companies see IT as an overhead and a significant cost factor; therefore, these companies seek to outsource their IT in the belief that it will be cheaper.

Below we show some examples of how widespread ITO is today. It seems that the trend is more likely to increase rather than decrease in the future.

- The IT budget going toward outsourcing has increased from an average of 10.6% in 2016 to an average of 11.9% in 2017, which is valued by Computer Economics Inc. 2017 as a "strong" increase.
- Ferranti (2016) referring to Gartner foresees that the global IT spending extension will increase from about 2% to 3% between 2017 and 2020.
- Flinders (2018) reports that the organizations in Europe, the Middle East and Africa increased their IT outsourcing expenditure in 2017. Globally, a new record for spending was set at €34.6bn for 2017.

The examples above describe the global ITO trend. Looking more specifically to the Nordic countries, it is noticeable that ITO is widely spread. For instance, 58% of the companies in Sweden and 76% in Denmark have outsourced their IT, (Ohnemus 2007). In another study conducted among the members of the CIO-Sweden association, it is mentioned that 70% of companies have outsourced their IT (CIOreporter 2012).

Lacity et al. (2008) conducted a study about outsourcing of back-office services. The authors used a research base of more than 500 companies located on five continents. They foresee that outsourcing will continue to be a high-risk business change with notable hidden costs, especially, in companies in which have adapted too slowly (Lacity et al. 2008). The authors also noted that this would happen in ITO contracts in which the service providers have low margins and the service buyers do not strategize, configure, monitor and manage their deals thoroughly. Therefore, in the authors' opinion, there will always be providers who will over-promise and under-deliver (Lacity et al. 2008). As estimated by Lacity et al. (2008), p. 28), "that just 50% of the large-scale contracts concerning complex processes which constitute more than 80% of the companies' operating budgets will be successful". Based on the study of Lacity et al. (2008) and their estimation, 30–50% of ITOs will not be relatively successful.

Ditmore (2012, p. 1) conducted a study which showed "Failed outsourcing deals, involving reputable vendors and customers, litter various industries". He also observed that companies are averse to making reports of their failures in ITO publicly available. Therefore, it is necessary to acquire accurate statistics[1]! As estimated by Ditmore (2012) at least 25% and probably more than half of this ITO will fail or perform very poorly.

Alexa Bona (2012) observed ITO problems. As a research director at Gartner she reported that hidden costs were not considered by the buying organization and therefore businesses frequently failed. She found that the outsourced IT operations became 30% more costly than the top quartile of the customer service operations conducted within the home organization. Of the service buyers aiming to outsource their customer management operations solely to cut costs, 80% failed. Bona (2012) also observed that 60% of companies who outsource parts of their customer-facing process must prepare to deal with customer defections and hidden costs. Therefore, in the opinion of Bona (2012), an outsourced service usually is more efficient, but then the sellers need to make a revenue too, which means that there is no money saving for the service buyer. It also has to be mentioned that the main reason for outsourcing IT was previously economic reasons. However, a study conducted in 2016 by PA Consulting and White Lane Research (2016) and carried out in the Nordic countries (Sweden, Norway, Denmark and Finland) found that the most frequent motivators for outsourcing IT are related to scalability, competence and flexibility. The mentioned study analyzed 1000 ITO contracts and found that in Sweden the access to IT resources is an essential motivator and that business transformation is the fastest-growing motivator. The study performed by PA Consulting and White Lane Research (2016) also revealed that 45% of the companies in Sweden expect to outsource more, and only 6% of the companies prefer to outsource less.

1.2   Research in IT Outsourcing in Large Companies: Research Problem, Motivation, and Goals

1.2.1   Research Problem

The research described in this book scrutinized IT outsourcing (ITO) from the buyer organizations' viewpoint with a focus on large companies. The main topics for the investigation have been (1) how to assess the ITO risks and mitigate them, (2) how to improve the ITO relationship between the outsourcer and the provider, (3) identify The research described in this book investigate IT outsourcing (ITO) from the buyer organizations' viewpoint with a focus on large companies. As the IT outsourcing concept is multidisciplinary, including IT management, strategic procurement, organizational, social, legal and economic theory and business administration together

---

[1]We recommend that before contracting the service buyer should seek references from previous or ongoing customers of the actual provider. This information could give valuable information about how their ITO has been handled by the potential supplier (Galliers and Leidner 2014).

with many interdependent IT tasks, contracts and projects. It makes ITO very complicated to study and to maximize successful outcomes. IT within organizations requires efficient ITO as IT is involved in nearly all business operations and therefore needs to run smoothly and reliably. The dynamic nature of ITO demands continuous evaluations and improvements of the operations, contracts and knowledge in the ITO field. The success factors of ITO. As the IT outsourcing concept is multidisciplinary, including IT management, strategic procurement, organizational, social, legal and economic theory and business administration together with many interdependent IT tasks, contracts and projects. It makes ITO very complicated to study and to maximize successful outcomes. IT within organizations requires efficient ITO as IT is involved in nearly all business operations and therefore needs to run smoothly and reliably. The dynamic nature of ITO demands continuous evaluations and improvements of the operations, contracts and knowledge in the ITO field.

IT has developed from giving basic administrative support to become an integral part of the business fundamentally supporting business strategies (Leonard and Seddon 2012). IT problems which occur in software, hardware, network, security are well known within companies and cause costly, troublesome delays. These problems are not solved by outsourcing IT. Additional complications may arise, because the provider and the buyer have their own interest which the process of negotiation may leave open to misunderstanding and a conflict of interests. It seems that two matters concerning ITO are assured:

- Outsourcing IT will remain problematic for the service buyer organizations (Frauenheim 2003; Lacity et al. 2008; Bona 2012; Ditmore 2012) and
- Outsourcing IT will remain and will expand in the future (Computer Economics Inc. 2017; Statista Inc. 2013).

Based on the evidence presented above, we can assume the following:

- Outsourcing IT will continue to be a business opportunity for the service buyers. In today's competitive industrial world, the demand for security solutions, IT competencies and resources demonstrates the fundamental value of IT for business in general.
- The high complexity of IT outsourcing ensures that ITO will continue to be a problem because of rapidly changing IT systems. These demand constant updates which will remain an expense and a challenge for the users to keep abreast of the new technology.

Another challenge to the improvement of ITO is IT service debasement as described by Aubert et al. (1998) and Schwarz et al. (2009). IT involvement in today's companies', in almost all business fields, could create delays or affect quality, which can cause the loss of customers' trust. Any IT and ITO problems affect the bottom line, in fact, ITO problems could incur significant financial losses for the organizations, which could crucially affect the competitive edge. It is well-documented that outsourcing IT is not always successful. Already 2003, Frauenheim (2003), estimated that 50% of the ITO would not bring the expected value. Also, other ITO researchers, like

Gonzalez et al. (2010), Overby (2013), Nicol (2014), Overby (2015) and Frydlinger (2016), observed comparable examples concerning unsuccessful ITO.

In summary we have found that a *considerable proportion of IT outsourcing is unsuccessful* as is referred to by the researchers mentioned above. In order to address this problem, this research aims to provide a new approach for improving ITO by focusing on risks, relationships and success factors in ITO. A description of the motivation to focus on risks, relationships and success factors in ITO will be explained in the next section.

1.2.2 Research Motivation

As was described in Sect. 1.2.1, a considerable proportion of IT outsourcing is unsuccessful which could create negative consequences for the organization that have outsourced IT or plan to do it. To address this problem we have chosen three perspectives: risks, relationships and success factors in ITO because they can address the problem of unsuccessful ITO. In our literature review about ITO, we found that a considerable number of research studies strive to reduce the unsuccessful ITOs by focusing on:

1. ITO risks (Kern and Willcocks 2002; Gonzalez et al. 2010; Lacity et al. 2010).
2. ITO relationships (Kern 1997; Gottschalk and Solli-Sæther 2006; Qi 2012; Qi and Chau 2012).
3. ITO success factors (Simmonds and Gilmour 2005; De Grahl 2012; Santos and Silva 2015).

Moreover, Liang et al. (2016) that have reviewed the ITO research literature published in the last 20 years identified the critical nodes that support the ITO knowledge flow. In their analyses Liang et al. (2016) have identified 12 major research themes, and among them there are the IT decisions, ITO risks and the relationship between buyer and provider. Furthermore, the authors have also identified ITO success as the next-in-line research theme that most researchers share as their main imperative goal. As we can see three of the research themes mentioned by Liang et al. (2016) are also the goals of this research that is in line with our research approach to address the research problem and improve ITO by focusing on the risks, relationships and success factors in ITO.

In the research we have performed the primary focus has been on buyer organizations that are large companies that have been explored in Sweden. However, as noticed, there is still a need to conduct more research on these topics concerning ITO that can be used by IT decision makers in large companies to improve their ITO.

However, as noticed, there is still a need to conduct more research on these topics concerning ITO that can be used by IT decision makers in large companies in Sweden to improve their ITO. As mentioned in Sect. 1.1, ITO will continue to increase in the near future, requiring new approaches that will improve ITO and reduce the number of unsuccessful implementations. In Sweden it has been observed that many large companies have used ITO as a business strategy and their intention is to use it in the near future (Frydlinger 2016). Therefore, there is still a need to analyse and define new ways to improve ITO to provide support for the IT decision makers in these companies. As mentioned in Sect. 1.1, ITO will continue to increase in the near future, requiring new approaches that will improve ITO and reduce the number of unsuccessful implementations. In Sweden it has been observed that many large companies have used ITO as a business strategy and their intention is to use it in the near future (Frydlinger 2016). Therefore, there is still a need to analyse and define new ways to improve ITO to provide support for the IT decision makers in these companies.

1.2.3 Research Goals

To address the research problem defined in Sect. 1.2.1, this study's main research goal (MRG) was to *analyse and define how to improve IT outsourcing (ITO) in large companies in Sweden considering the buyer organization.*

To achieve the main research goal, we have formulated three research goals (RGs) that are the followings:

RG1: To develop a method for risk assessment in IT outsourcing.
RG2: To identify the important factors in IT outsourcing relationships.
RG3: To identify the success factors in IT outsourcing.

A short description of the research goals contributing to the main research goal is presented below.

RG1 aimed to develop a method for assessing the risks to support IT decision makers in their decision on whether to outsource IT or not. This method enables IT decision makers to assess ongoing IT outsourcing by evaluating the risks and proposing how to mitigate them. Using the method, IT decisions makers can assess the ITO risks. If they plan to outsource their IT, then the method could lead them to postpone their action until the greatest risks have been mitigated. If the IT has already been outsourced, then the method could guide the IT decision makers in mitigating the risks. The method can help them to improve their ITO and reduce the number of unsuccessful ITOs.

RG2 aimed to identify the important factors in IT outsourcing relationships to support the service buyer organization. Kern and Willcocks (2002, p. 3) describe a "relationship" as "The state of being connected or related; the mutual dealings, connections, or feelings that exist between two parties". As noticed, the relationship between the ITO buyer and the provider(s) is a prerequisite for successful ITO. Therefore, this research goal was to analyse and identify the most important factors in the ITO relationship in large companies in Sweden and define a priority list of these factors.

RG3 aimed to identify the success factors in IT outsourcing. Success factors (SFs) are those factors that could improve IT outsourcing (Leimeister and Krcmar 2004;

Hodosi et al. 2015). Accomplishing RG3, we develop a list of success factors, create a prioritized list according to their importance. By using these SFs, the number of unsuccessful ITOs could be reduced.

1.3 Delimitations

The research presented in this book has focused on large companies with representation in Sweden that have outsourced their IT. Large companies are those that have 250 or more employees, according to Ekonomifakta (2014). In one research study, large companies are also compared with medium-sized companies, which have 50–249 employees (Ekonomifakta 2014).

The studied large companies, have subsidiaries with IT planning and development outside Sweden. These companies have an IT department with a Chief Information Officer (CIO) or equivalent position, and the respondents from these companies have internal access (within the company) to relevant expertise in their support departments, such as sourcing, contracting and quality management.

In the definition of IT outsourcing arrangements given by Gartner (2016), which was introduced in Sect. 1.1, the software development is excluded, as well as business processes that are not IT related. For example, IT operations and development and maintenance of the IT used in the case of the outsourcing of a call centre (like healthcare) are included in this definition but not necessarily the way in which the work is performed to operate the call centre (like giving medical advice). Therefore, this research only considered IT outsourcing of services. Additionally, software development is excluded, but not small adaptations and integrations.

Cloud solutions, like cloud computing (cloud sourcing), which is a method of computing in which flexible capabilities are delivered as a service using Internet technologies (Gartner 2016), were not included in this study, because the focus of the research was on "traditional" ITO.

Moreover, the research performed did not investigate specifically business process outsourcing (BPO), that is, the outsourcing of business processes according to Lacity et al. (2011, p. 221). If the service buyer has outsourced all or parts of its IT or any complete or partial IT-based processes (like logistics or enterprise resource planning), this research did not differentiate the outsourcing types.

Furthermore, the research performed in this book did not distinguish between single outsourcing and multi-vendor outsourcing (or just multi-sourcing), which, according to Feng (2012), is a type of IT outsourcing that involves contracting several providers, in our case IT services.

In summary, the research undertaken in this book explored large companies in Sweden. Moreover, it considered only IT services, excluding large IT application developments but including smaller adaptations like tuning, configuring of IT applications and infrastructure.

References

Aubert, B., Patry, M., & Rivard, S. (1998). Assessing the risk of IT outsourcing. In *Proceedings of 31st Annual Hawaii International Conference on System Sciences*. Waikoloa, HI: IEEE Computer Society.

Bona, A. (2012). *Gartner: Customer service outsourcing costs more than in-house*. Todd Bouldin Enterprises, LLC. Accessed May 1, 2018, from https://toddbouldin.com/2012/03/19/gartner-customer-service-outsourcing-costs-more-than-in-house

CIOreporter. (2012). *70 procent har delar av it-avdelningen outsourcad – men bara 47 procent har en sourcingstrategi*. CIO Sweden, IDG. Accessed May 1, 2018, from http://cio.idg.se/2.1782/1.449100/cioernas-outsourcing-i-siffror

Computer Economics Inc. (2017). *IT outsourcing statistics 2017/2018*. ISBN 0-945052-92-8, ISBN 1-56909-010-6. Accessed May 1, 2018, from http://www.computereconomics.com

De Grahl, A. (2012). *Success factors in logistics outsourcing*. Wiesbaden: Gabler (Springer Fachmedien).

Ditmore, J. (2012). *Why IT outsourcing often fails information week*. Global CIO. Accessed May 1, 2018, from http://www.informationweek.com/global-cio/interviews/why-it-outsourcing-often-fails/240003659

Ekonomifakta. (2014). *Företagens storlek*. Accessed May 1, 2018, from http://www.ekonomifakta.se/sv/Fakta/Foretagande/Naringslivet/Naringslivets-struktur/

Feng, B. (2012). Multisourcing suppliers selection in service outsourcing. *Journal of the Operational Research Society, 63*(5), 582–596. https://doi.org/10.1057/jors.2011.6.

Ferranti, M. (2016). *Global spending on tech will be more or less flat this year and not much better through 2020*. InfoWorld. Accessed May 1, 2018, from http://www.infoworld.com/article/3053611/cloud-computing/slow-growth-ahead-for-it-spending-gartner-says.html

Flinders, K. (2018). *Demand for cloud services drives increase in IT outsourcing*. Tech Target, Computer Weekly. Accessed May 1, 2018, from http://www.computerweekly.com/news/450433419/Demand-for-cloud-services-drives-increase-in-IT-outsourcing

Frauenheim, E. (2003). *IT outsourcing will disappoint*. Gartner. Accessed May 1, 2018, from http://news.com.com/Gartner+IT+outsourcing+will+disappoint/2100-1011_3-994108.html

Frydlinger, D. (2016). *Spara pengar och vinn innovation på bättre skrivna outsourcingkontrakt*. Stockholm: International Data Group. Accessed May 1, 2018, from http://computersweden.idg.se/2.2683/1.656619/outsourcing-kontrakt.

Galliers, R., & Leidner, D. (2014). *Strategic information management: Challenges and strategies in managing information systems* (4th ed.). London: Routledge. ISBN13: 9781134730193.

Gartner Inc. (2016). *IT glossary*. Gartner, Inc. Accessed May 1, 2018, from http://www.gartner.com/it-glossary/?s=it+outsourcing

Gonzalez, R., Gasco, J., & Llopis, J. (2010). Information systems outsourcing reasons and risks: A new assessment. *Industrial Management & Data Systems, 110*(2), 284–303.

Gottschalk, P., & Solli-Sæther, H. (2006). *Managing successful IT outsourcing relationships*. Hershey, PA: IRM Press.

Hodosi, G., Kaye, R., & Rusu, L. (2015). IT outsourcing success factors: A study of large and medium-sized companies. In S. Gao & L. Rusu (Eds.), *Modern techniques for successful IT project management* (pp. 183–199). Hershey, PA: IGI Global.

Kern, T. (1997). The Gestalt of an information technology outsourcing relationship: An exploratory analysis. In *Proceedings of the Eighteenth International Conference on Information Systems (ICIS 1997)* (pp. 37–58). Atlanta, GA: Association for Information Systems.

Kern, T., & Willcocks, L. (2002). Exploring relationships in information technology outsourcing: The interaction approach. *European Journal of Information Systems, 11*, 3–19.

Lacity, M., Willcocks, L., & Rottman, J. (2008). Global outsourcing of back office services: Lessons, trends, and enduring challenges. *Strategic Outsourcing: An International Journal, 1*(1), 13–34.

Lacity, M. C., Khan, S., Yan, A., & Willcocks, L. P. (2010). A review of the IT outsourcing empirical literature and future research directions. *Journal of Information Technology, 25*(4), 395–433.

Lacity, M., Solomon, S., Yan, A., & Willcocks, L. (2011). Business process outsourcing studies: A critical review and research directions. *Journal of Information Technology, 26,* 221–258.

Leimeister, S. (2010). *IT outsourcing governance: Client types and their management strategies.* Wiesbaden: Gabler.

Leimeister, J., & Krcmar, H. (2004). Success factors of virtual communities from the perspective of members and operators: An empirical study. In *Proceedings of the 37th Annual Hawaii International Conference on System Sciences (HICSS'04)* (pp. 1–10). Washington, DC: IEEE Computer Society.

Leonard, J., & Seddon, P. (2012). A meta-model of alignment. *Communications of the Association for Information Systems, 31*(1), 230–259.

Liang, H., Wang, J., Xue, Y., & Cui, X. (2016). IT outsourcing research from 1992 to 2013: A literature review based on main path analysis. *Information & Management, 53*(2), 227–251.

Nicol, A. (2014). *How outsourcing went horribly wrong.* Product Design & Development. Accessed May 1, 2018, from http://www.pddnet.com/blog/2014/01/how-outsourcing-went-horribly-wrong

Ohnemus, J. (2007). *Does IT outsourcing increase firm success? An empirical assessment using firm-level data* (pp. 1–56). Discussion Paper No. 07-087, Centre for European Economic Research (ZEW), Mannheim, Germany. Accessed May 1, 2016, from http://ftp.zew.de/pub/zew-docs/dp/dp07087.pdf

Overby, S. (2013). *10 steps to ensure your IT outsourcing deal fails.* CIO from IDG. Accessed May 1, 2018, from http://www.cio.com/article/2382183/outsourcing/10-steps-to-ensure-your-it-outsourcing-deal-fails.htm

Overby, S. (2015). *Federal IT outsourcing is alarmingly poorly managed* [online]. InfoWorld. Accessed May 1, 2018, from http://www.infoworld.com/article/2999833/outsourcing/federal-it-outsourcing-is-alarmingly-poorly-managed.html

PA Consulting and White Lane Research. (2016). 4 trender inom IT-outsourcing i Sverige. In *2016 Nordic IT outsourcing.* Accessed May 1, 2018, from http://www.idenet.com/se/blogg/cio-insikt/327-it-outsourcing-sverige

Qi, C. (2012). Relationship and contract issues of IT outsourcing – An empirical study in China. In *Proceedings of Americas Conference on Information Systems (AMCIS)* (Paper 4). Seattle, WA: Association for Information Systems.

Qi, C., & Chau, P. (2012). Relationship, contract and IT outsourcing success: Evidence from two descriptive case studies. *Decision Support Systems, 53,* 859–869.

Santos, J., & Silva, M. (2015). Mapping critical success factors for IT outsourcing: The providers' perspective. *International Journal of Enterprise Information Systems, 11*(1), 62–84.

Schwarz, A., Jayatilaka, B., Hirschheim, R., & Goles, T. (2009). A conjoint approach to understanding IT application services outsourcing. *Journal of the Association for Information Systems, 10*(1), 187–201.

Simmonds, A., & Gilmour, D. (2005). *IT governance domain practices and competences, governance of outsourcing.* Accessed May 1, 2018, from http://www.itgi.org

Statista Inc. (2013). *Outsourcing – Global market size 2012.* Accessed May 1, 2018, from http://www.statista.com/statistics/189788/global-outsourcing-market-size-since-2000

Chapter 2
Research Background

Abstract In this chapter are described IT outsourcing services, IT outsourcing types, total versus selective IT outsourcing, single versus multiple providers, and how to select IT outsourcing provider. Additionally, this chapter includes the theories in IT outsourcing used in this research and also the risks, relationships and success factors in IT outsourcing that are our research goals.

Keywords IT outsourcing services · IT outsourcing types · Cloud solutions · IT outsourcing provider · Transaction cost theory · Risks · Important factors · Success factors

2.1 IT Outsourcing Background

In this section are described the most important IT outsourcing concepts for our research.

2.1.1 IT Outsourcing Services

First of all is good to mention that IT outsourcing should support the efficient use of IT in all business areas for the service buyer organizations (Hodosi and Rusu 2013). According to Beulen (2011) IT outsourcing services are referring to the applications and infrastructure management. In opinion of Beulen (2011) the primary activities in application management are the followings: 1) maintaining the applications; 2) bug fixing; and 3) improving and adjusting the application according to process change requests. In fact, application management contains two types of applications, standard software and dedicated software. Examples of application standard software are packages such as management information systems (MIS), enterprise resource planning (ERP) and database management software as commercial off-the-shelf

G. Hodosi, L. Rusu, *Risks, Relationships and Success Factors in IT Outsourcing*,
SpringerBriefs in Information Systems,
https://doi.org/10.1007/978-3-030-05925-5_2

(COTS) software. As Beulen (2011) noticed, standard applications are implemented and frequently modified to meet the specific requirement of the clients, while the dedicated software application is developed with a particular specification for each IT outsourcing buyer. Specific knowledge is also necessary both to develop and to maintain such software. Concerning the infrastructure management this includes the server, network management systems and the desktop. The interaction with the service buyer requires less interaction and vicinity to the outsourcers' location than the application management (Beulen et al. 2005).

2.1.2   Total Versus Selective IT Outsourcing

Outsourcing of IT can be done totally, which means that the whole IT service is performed externally, or selectively, where just parts of the IT are outsourced, for example outsource the network and keep infrastructure and applications in-house.

Total outsourcing is rare, as most companies retain at least a small part of the IT personnel. Hirscheim et al. (2006, p. 110) define total outsourcing as follows: "80% or more of the IT budget is made up of costs for IT services". "Complete outsourcing" is used as a synonym for "total outsourcing". Furthermore, some companies perform almost all their IT activity internally while purchasing just a small number of applications. The definition of total insourcing is a company spending 80% or more of the budget for IT services internally. But in selective ITO we should have at least 20% but less than 80% of the IT budget that is outsourced. In the research we have performed we noticed that all the respondents have mentioned that their companies have practiced the selective ITO.

2.1.3   Single Versus Multiple Providers

Large companies can select more than one provider, for example one provider that takes responsibility for the infrastructure and another that takes care of the applications, or divide the IT services geographically by city, country or continent. The advantages for the service buyer are the access to the best of breed, the risk division (for example, three parties instead of two parties), the lower level of dependency on the provider and the competition among the providers. The disadvantage is to have higher transaction costs because there are several contracts to manage (Lacity et al. 2008). In fact is very common to use more providers and most of our respondents in our research have used two providers.

2.1.4   IT Outsourcing Provider Selection

This topic has been studied for many years, mostly in the scope of supply chain management (Weber et al. 1991; Cao and Wang 2007; Ho et al. 2010; Karami et al.

2010). Here we only recapitulate some issues, more specific to ITO, containing sensitive data. In addition to performing well (which also includes financial stability), using state of the art technology, right price, just to mention some vendor requirements, the service buyer's business has to be protected. For this reason the outsourcer should consider the following questions:

- Does the provider take enough measures to protect the outsourcer's data?
- If the provider also handles the outsourcer's competitors, does the provider take appropriate measures to protect your data?
- Ifs the service buyer's data is not handled locally, does the abroad data get the same protection as locally? This regards both human and IT resources. National security data should not be transferred abroad.
- Are the rights to spontaneously audit the security contractually confirmed?

Therefore we think that the questions mentioned above should be treated as the main requirements for a provider selection. Additionally, the buyer should contact the potential provider's customers! This enables to get informed about the provider's service delivery, ITO relationship quality, price development, and the provider's ability to change, just to mention some of the essential topics.

2.2 Theories in IT Outsourcing

This section describes the theories in IT outsourcing that we have used in our research.

2.2.1 Transaction Cost Theory

Despite that transaction cost theory (TCT) have originated several decades ago, the theory is still used by several researchers within ITO: to mention only a few of them like Bahli and Rivard (2013), Christ et al. (2014), Solli-Sæther and Gottschalk (2015), Dibbern et al. (2016), Schermann et al. (2016) and Tiwana and Kim (2016).

In 2009 Williamson (1985) received the "Sveriges Riksbank Prize in Economic Sciences in, Memory of Alfred Nobel" for the developed TCT. Moreover, according to Nyrhinen and Dahlberg (2007), TCT is the most authoritative theory used for outsourcing analysis. Furthermore, as Williamson (1985, p. 41) states, "Any problem that can be posed directly or indirectly as a contracting problem is usefully investigated in transaction cost economizing terms", and ITO is especially concerned with the contracting problem. Therefore, the use of TCT does not have to be justified. In summary, TCT covers the whole life cycle from the preparation of ITO (ex-ante) to the implemented phase (ex-post) and includes the necessary factors for contracting and the ITO relationship. The completeness makes TCT the best choice for this research compared with other theories used in ITO research, like core competency theory, agency theory and the research-based view. For specific problems, for example asymmetric information, agency theory can provide deeper knowledge or, when the needed competence is unclear, the core competence theory could help the researcher to address this issue.

2.2.2 Agency Theory

Agency theory (AT) is a general theory used in economic, political and social science and treats the difficulties that arise under conditions of incomplete and asymmetric information. In AT information is regarded as a commodity (Eisenhardt 1989). The principal has to invest in obtaining information to be able to monitor its agent. Applied to ITO, AT helps to understand the problems that could occur when the principal is the service buyer organization and the agent the service provider. The incentive system in AT is the avoidance of conflicts between the buyer and the provider. AT is more strongly focused on contracts than TCT. Both parties wish to create incentives to avoid efficiency losses. Actually, the principal and the agent have different interests, known as the "buyer–seller dilemma", as described by Kacprzyk et al. (2012, p. 232). Additionally, regarding risk sharing, when the buyer and the provider have different attitudes towards risk, the actions to be taken will differ and can cause conflicts (Eisenhardt 1989, p. 58). The real problems arise with opportunistic behaviour, which is enhanced by information asymmetry and the fact that the individuals in each company can act for their own individual interests (Hodosi 2010). Agency theory is a commonly used theory in research on conflicts of interest, motivation problems and mechanisms for managing incentive problems (Guilding et al. 2005). It has to be mentioned that there are two different sides to the interpretation of AT. One side emphasizes that AT covers how capital markets can affect firms; the other side does not see this limitation and supports generalized use.

2.2.3 Core Competency Theory

Core competency theory (CCT) analyses the firm's functions to explore which activities can be performed cost-effectively by keeping them in-house and those activities that could be outsourced (Jensen and Meckling 1976). Core competencies are the capabilities that are critical for the business to attain its competitive advantage. The CCT guides the service-buying company to concentrate on the core competencies and not to outsource them but instead to keep them in-house as a unique asset. Prahalad and Hamel (1990) present the main concepts of core competencies and have recommended that activities that are recognized as core competencies should be kept in-house. Other activities, that is, the rest, should be achieved with the best providers that are available. However, some activities that are non-core but contribute to the delivery of a competitive advantage for the company should not be outsourced (Gottschalk and Solli-Sæther 2006). As the product portfolio changes, the core and non-core competencies have to be re-evaluated. Information technology is a central tool for all development, nowadays; therefore, therefore CCT becomes a critical issue and a central theory in ITO.

2.2.4   Resource-Based Theory

Companies are viewed as collections of competencies and capabilities that must be maintained and developed. The focus of resource-based theory (RBT) is on internal characteristics as factors of companies' competitive success. According to Cumps et al. (2006, p. 2), "The logic is that a sustainable competitive advantage can be created when there is resource heterogeneity (resources are different across organizations) and resource immobility (competitors find it hard to imitate or substitute these resources)". Moreover, RBT explains why some companies obtain a strategic advantage and others do not and, while some firms are able to maintain the strategic advantage, others are not. It also gives an indication about whether an activity should be outsourced or kept inside the company. These two properties make RBT a useful theory for decision makers regarding the question of whether to outsource or not. More precisely, RBT focuses on the strategic resources that the company develops and sustains and that are essential to the development of a strategic advantage (Barney 1991). RBT is based on the following prerequisites: 1) history matters: the companies are bounded by their former choices; 2) resources are not perfectly mobile; and 3) expertise is not easy to reproduce or imitate. In fact, measuring tacit knowledge it is difficult. Therefore, this lack obstructs the management in handling this issue correctly.

2.3   Risks, Relationships and Success Factors in IT Outsourcing

In this section we describe the risks, relationships and success factors in IT outsourcing that we have explored in our research.

2.3.1   Risks

Deciding whether to outsource IT or not is a complex task containing many risks that must be identified and analyzed. The risks have to be compared to determine which problems should be addressed to mitigate the overall risks. Most of the ITO decisions have time and budget constraints that limit a detailed analysis. ITO is a one-time process, and identifying all the risk areas for the first time is a huge challenge (Hodosi 2010). When IT is outsourced, the work with risk mitigation remains and issues like cost reduction are still a challenge. According to Boehm (1991, p. 35), the risk for an ITO scenario is "the possibility of loss or injury". This means that in this context the risk "either refers to the probability of negative outcomes or factors that lead to the negative outcomes" (Corbitt and Tho 2005, p. 2). Moreover, risk has several technical uses according to Hansson (2007, p. 1), such as:

- An unwanted event that may or may not occur (Hansson 2007, p. 1), for example a "loss of revenue is one of the major risks that affects unsuccessful IT outsourcing", as observed by Rusu and Hodosi (2011, p. 27).
- The cause of an unwanted event that may or may not occur (Hansson 2007, p. 1), for example "the losses of the revenues are mostly caused by additional time and costs for IT", as observed by Rusu and Hodosi (2011, p. 27). The unwanted event is the problem caused by unsuccessful ITO, which means more work costs and effort. The previous and actual bullets are a qualitative sense of risk.
- The probability of an unwanted event, that may or may not occur (Hansson 2007, p. 1), for example "the risk that the ITO is unsuccessful regarding keeping losses of revenue at about 50%", as observed by Rusu and Hodosi (2011, p. 27). Here, we have a quantitative sense of risk.

The statistical expectation value of an unwanted event that may or may not occur, such as "The expectation value of a possible negative event is the product of its probability and some measure of its severity" (Hansson 2007, p. 1). According to Ostrom and Wilhelmsen (2012), severity is described as the degree of something undesirable, and this interpretation will be used in this book. Applied to ITO, this could be severe regarding losses, a business critical situation or underperformed services, just to mention a few problems.

The method developed for assessing the risks in ITO (that is one of our research goals) has used the last interpretation of the risk calculation. According to the ISO/IEC Guide 73:2002 (ISO 2002), a risk is a combination of the probability of an event and its consequence. This standard uses both potential parts of the events: the beneficial part, that is, opportunities, and the threat part, namely unintended consequences. It is assumed that the international standard ISO/IEC Guide 73:2002 has broad usage among corporate and public organizations. In this book, to assess the risk exposure, the threat part, namely potential losses, is used and the risk exposure is defined as "The quantified potential for loss that might occur as a result of some activity" (Murcko 2014). In fact, risk exposure (RE) is a simple calculation that gives a numeric value to risk and that enables users to compare different risks; it is calculated with the following formula:

Risk exposure$_i$ of any given risk $= RE_i =$ (probability$_i$ of risk occurring) $\times$ (loss$_i$ if the risk occurs);

Total risk exposure $= RE_1 + RE_2 + RE_3 + \ldots RE_n; [1..n]$

The formula calculates the REs using the probabilities and losses of the risk occurring. By calculating the REs, IT decision makers can analyse the ITO risks in the following way: giving a numeric value to the risks enables them to compare the different ITO risks. The different risk exposures can be accumulated and compared with the ITO decision makers' accepted risk exposure. Moreover, the IT decision makers can use a prioritized risk list that could guide them in their risk-planning activities.

The research literature contains several ITO risk frameworks. The one selected for this research is that of Bahli and Rivard (2002) because it fits best with the scenarios used for the developed decision model implemented in the method for assessment of risks in ITO (ITODSM).

2.3.2 IT Outsourcing Relationships

ITO research uses a broad vocabulary to define the different factors that influence outsourcing relationships. Some examples are attributes, ITO relationships, relationship factors, behavioural factors, dimensions, key factors, important factors in ITO relationships and determinants of outsourcing success. The attributes of a successful ITO relationship are used by researchers such as Alborz et al. (2005), Sargent (2006) and Jahyun Goo and Nam (2007), but no research studies define the attributes, rather using them as success factors, and a lack of the attributes can cause "un-success factors".

The importance of seriously addressing the partnership in the ITO management has been studied for example by Fitzgerald and Willcocks (1994) and Kern and Willcocks (2002), some decades ago.

It also has to be mentioned, that there is no definitive answer to the question of "how to develop and maintain a successful relationship", and Kern and Willcocks (2000) mention "gut feelings" instead of a policy.

Moreover, in the opinion of Hirscheim et al. (2006), relationship management is an important issue for successful IT outsourcing, an opinion that is shared by other researchers, like Goo (2009) and Lee et al. (2009).

2.3.3 Success Factors in IT Outsourcing

In many leading research journals, the terminology "Success Factors" has not been clearly defined and it seems to be a consensus that the term is well understood in the research community. On the other hand and precisely for this study Benbasat and Zmud (1999, p. 5) have suggested that to be relevant for IT, research should be conducted to serve IT professionals and also "... provide real value to IS professionals". Therefore we believe that Success Factors (SFs) are in general, easy to understand by the IT professionals.

In the opinion of Rockart (1979, p. 85) Critical Success Factors (CSF) are defined as "the limited number of areas in which results if they are satisfactory, will ensure successful competitive performance for the organization". According to Rockart (1979, p. 85), "the critical success factors are areas of activity that should receive constant and careful attention from management". Considering this definition of CSF and apply it in the case of CSF in IT outsourcing, we could say that this means, that within a regular interval it is a need to evaluate those CSFs that will be implemented, and which will due to the improvement of the actual ITO.

References

Alborz, S., Seddon, P., & Scheepers, R. (2005). The quality-of-relationship construct in IT outsourcing. In *PACIS 2005 proceedings,* Paper 93, Association for Information Systems.

Bahli, B., & Rivard, S. (2002). Information technology outsourcing risk: A scenario-based conceptualisation. *Cahier de la Chaire de gestion stratégique des technologies de l'information:* HEC Montréal, 3000, chemin de la Côte-Sainte-Catherine, Montréal, Québec, H3T 2A7 Canada, no 02–04 – Octobre 2002, ISSN 1702-238X, 1–22. Accessed May 1, 2018, from http://neumann.hec.ca/chairegestionti/cahiers/cahier0204.pdf

Bahli, B., & Rivard, S. (2013). Cost escalation in information technology outsourcing: A moderated mediation study. *Decision Support Systems, 56,* 37–47.

Barney, J. (1991). Firm resources and sustained competitive advantage. *Journal of Management, 17* (1), 99–120.

Benbasat, I., & Zmud, R. (1999). Empirical research in information systems: The practice of relevance. *MIS Quarterly, 23*(1), 3–16.

Beulen, E. (2011). Maturing IT outsourcing relationships: A transaction costs perspective. In J. Kotlarsky, L. Willcocks, & I. Oshri (Eds.), *New studies in global IT and business service outsourcing: Lecture notes in business information processing* (pp. 66–79). Berlin: Springer.

Beulen, E., Fenema, P., & Currie, W. (2005). From application outsourcing to infrastructure management: Extending the offshore outsourcing service portfolio. *European Management Journal, 23*(2), 133–144.

Boehm, B. (1991). Software risk management: Principles and practices. *IEEE Software, 8,* 32–42.

Cao, Q., & Wang, Q. (2007). Optimizing vendor selection in a two-stage outsourcing process. *Computers & Operations Research, 34*(12), 3757–3768.

Christ, M., Mintchik, N., Chen, L., & Bierstaker, J. (2014). Outsourcing the information system: Determinants, risks, and implications for management control systems. *Journal of Management Accounting Research, 27*(2), 77–120.

Corbitt, B., & Tho, I. (2005). Towards an economic analysis of IT outsourcing risks. In *Proceedings 16th Australasian conference on information systems* (pp. 1–8). Sydney: Association for Information Systems.

Cumps, B., Viaene, S., Dedene, G., & Vandenbulcke, J. (2006). A theoretical exploration of the relationship between outsourcing and business/ICT alignment. In *Proceedings of European conference on information systems (ECIS 2006).* Gothenburg: Association for Information Systems.

Dibbern, J., Chin, W., & Kude, T. (2016). The sourcing of software services: Knowledge specificity and the role of trust. *SIGMIS Database, 47*(2), 36–57.

Eisenhardt, K. (1989). Agency theory: An assessment and review. *Academy of Management Review, 14*(1), 57–74.

Fitzgerald, F., & Willcocks, L. (1994). Contracts and partnerships in the outsourcing of IT. In *Proceedings of fifteenth international conference on information systems* (pp. 51–63). Vancouver, British Columbia: Association for Information Systems.

Goo, J. (2009). Promoting trust and relationship commitment through service level agreements in IT outsourcing relationship. In R. Hirscheim, A. Heinzl, & J. Dibbern (Eds.), *Information systems outsourcing enduring themes, global challenges, and process opportunities* (3rd ed., pp. 27–53). Heidelberg: Springer.

Gottschalk, P., & Solli-Sæther, H. (2006). *Managing successful IT outsourcing relationships*. Hershey, PA: IRM Press.

Guilding, C., Warnken, J., Ardill, A., & Fredline, L. (2005). An agency theory perspective on the owner/manager relationship in tourism-based condominiums. *Tourism Management, 26*(3), 409–420.

Hansson, S. (2007). Risk. In E. Zalta (Ed.), *Stanford encyclopedia of philosophy* (Winter 2008 Edition). Accessed May 1, 2018, from http://plato.stanford.edu/archives/win2008/entries/risk/

Hirscheim, R., Heinzl, A., & Dibbern, J. (2006). *Information systems outsourcing, enduring themes, new perspectives and global challenges* (2nd ed.). Berlin: Springer.

Ho, W., Xu, X., & Dey, P. (2010). Multi-criteria decision making approaches for supplier evaluation and selection: A literature review. *European Journal of Operational Research, 202*(1), 16–24.

Hodosi, G. (2010). A method for decision support in information technology outsourcing: The case for large Swedish companies. Licentiate Thesis, Report Series No. 10–003, ISSN 1101–8526, 2010, Stockholm University, Stockholm.

Hodosi, G., & Rusu, L. (2013). How do critical success factors contribute to a successful IT outsourcing: A study of large multinational companies. *Journal of Information Technology Theory and Application (JITTA), 14*(1), 17–43.

ISO. (2002). *SO/IEC guide 73:2002, risk management – Vocabulary – Guidelines for use in standards*. Accessed May 1, 2018, from http://www.iso.org/iso/catalogue_detail?csnumber=34998

Jahyun Goo, J., & Nam, K. (2007). Contract as a source of trust–commitment in successful IT outsourcing relationship: An empirical study. In *Proceedings of the 40th annual Hawaii international conference on system sciences* (pp. 1–10). Washington, DC: IEEE Computer Society.

Jensen, M., & Meckling, W. (1976). Theory of the firm: Managerial behavior, agency costs and ownership structure. *Journal of Financial Economics, Harvard University Press, 3*(4), 305–360.

Kacprzyk, J., Nurmi, H., & Fedrizzi, M. (2012). *Consensus under fuzziness*. New York: Springer Science & Business Media.

Karami, A., Yazdani, H., Beiryaie, H., & Hosseinzadeh, N. (2010). A risk based model for IS outsourcing vendor selection. In *2010 2nd IEEE international conference on information and financial engineering, Chongqing* (pp. 250–254). Piscataway, NJ: IEEE.

Kern, T., & Willcocks, L. (2000). Exploring information technology outsourcing relationships: Theory and practice. *Journal of Strategic Information Systems, 9*(4), 321–350.

Kern, T., & Willcocks, L. (2002). Exploring relationships in information technology outsourcing: The interaction approach. *European Journal of Information Systems, 11*, 3–19.

Lacity, M., Willcocks, L., & Rottman, J. (2008). Global outsourcing of back office services: Lessons, trends, and enduring challenges. *Strategic Outsourcing: An International Journal, 1*(1), 13–34.

Lee, J., Huynh, M., & Hirscheim, R. (2009). Exploring the role of initial trust, initial distrust, and trust through knowledge sharing in IT outsourcing: From a service receiver's perspective. In R. Hirscheim, A. Heinzl, & J. Dibbern (Eds.), *Information systems outsourcing enduring themes, global challenges, and process opportunities* (3rd ed., pp. 55–74). Berlin: Springer.

Murcko, T. (2014). *BusinessDictionary – online*. WebFinance, Inc. Accessed April 1, 2018, from http://www.businessdictionary.com/definition/risk-exposure.html

Nyrhinen, M., & Dahlberg, T. (2007). Is transaction cost theory able to explain contracts used for and success of firm-wide IT-infrastructure outsourcing? In *Proceedings of the 40th Hawaii international conference on system sciences (HICSS-40)*. Waikoloa, HI: IEEE Computer Society.

Ostrom, L., & Wilhelmsen, C. (2012). *Risk assessment, tools, techniques, and their applications*. Hoboken, NJ: Wiley.

Prahalad, C., & Hamel, G. (1990). The core competence of the corporation. *Harvard Business Review, 68*(3), 79–91.

Rockart, J. (1979). Chief executives define their own data needs. *Harvard Business Review, 57*(2), 81–94.

Rusu, L., & Hodosi, G. (2011). Assessing the risk exposure in IT outsourcing for large companies. *International Journal of Information Technology and Management, 10*(1), 24–44.

Sargent, A. (2006). Outsourcing relationship literature: An examination and implications for future research. In *Proceedings of the 2006 ACM SIGMIS CPR conference on computer personnel research: Forty four years of computer personnel research: Achievements, challenges & the future* (pp. 280–287). New York: Association for Computing Machinery.

Schermann, M., Dongus, K., Yetton, P., & Krcmar, H. (2016). The role of transaction cost economics in information technology outsourcing research: A meta-analysis of the choice of contract type. *The Journal of Strategic Information Systems, 25*(1), 32–48.

Solli-Sæther, H., & Gottschalk, P. (2015). Stages-of-growth in outsourcing, offshoring and backsourcing: Back to the future? *Journal of Computer Information Systems, 55*(2), 88–94.

Tiwana, A., & Kim, S. (2016). Concurrent IT sourcing: Mechanisms and contingent advantages. *Journal of Management Information Systems, 33*(1), 1–38.

Weber, C., Current, J., & Benton, W. (1991). Vendor selection criteria and methods. *European Journal of Operational Research, 50*(1), 2–18.

Williamson, O. (1985). *The economic institutions of capitalism – Firms, markets, relational contracting*. London: The Free Press.

Chapter 3
Research Process

Abstract This chapter describes the research process that includes the applied research strategies and methods used for achieving the research goals. The activities performed for achieving research goal 1 (a method for risk assessment in ITO), and research 2 (to identify the important factors in the ITO relationship) have been performed in large companies, while the activities for research goal 3 (to identify the success factors in ITO) have been performed in both large and medium-sized companies.

Keywords IT outsourcing · Research process · Research strategy · Research method · Risk factors · Relationships factors · Success factors

3.1 Applied Research Strategies and Methods

The applied research strategies to achieve the research goals are design science research and survey research. Design Science Research (DSR) has been applied because it supports the development and evaluation of a new IT artefact, usually, a solution to an identified organizational issue (Hevner et al. 2004). The developed artefact is a method named IT outsourcing decision support method (ITODSM). The other applied research strategy in this research is survey research, because it ensures broad and comprehensive coverage (Denscombe 2010) to study ITO risks, relationships and success factors in large companies in Sweden. At a specific time, this strategy enabled the researcher to bring matters "up to date" and provide information about the current states of ITO in the studied companies. Bhattacherjee (2012) notes that survey research is best suited to studies that have units of analysis consisting of groups/organizations or pairs of organizations, such as buyers and sellers, as are in our study. Concerning the data collection methods used to achieve the three research goals these were interviews, questionnaires, documents, web information and e-mails while the research method used for data analyses was thematic analysis.

The applied research strategies and methods to achieve each of the research goals (RGs) are presented in Table 3.1.

The research performed to achieve the three research goals including the data collection in large companies in Sweden has been done during two periods of time. The first period of time is named Study 1, and this study has been performed between 2007 and 2014. The second period of time is named Study 2, and the research performed in this study has been done between 2015 and February 2016. The data collection in both studies was done by using the same questionnaires and interview questions. The number of large companies and the number of respondents per each study in each of these studies is shown in Table 3.2.

The conducted studies were done in mainly large companies from different business segments like Oil & Gas, Basic Materials, Industrials, Consumer Services, Consumer Goods, Financials, Health Care and Technology. This spread of the sectors covers most of the industries and enables to generalize the research findings to a broad industry segment. Furthermore, the respondents in these companies have different IT management positions like e.g. Project Manager, IT service Manager, IT Director, IT Solution Manager, Head of IT Department, Vice- President for IT, and Chief Information Officer, just to mention some of them. The spread regarding the business sectors of the studied companies and the IT decision makers' position has enabled a representative sampling for the group of mostly large companies in Sweden.

Table 3.1 Research strategies and methods applied to achieve the research goals

Research goals/ research strategies and methods	Research goal 1 (RG1)	Research goal 2 (RG2)	Research goal 3 (RG3)
Research strategies	Design science research for the development of a method for risk assessment in ITO. Survey research to identify the risk factors in ITO	Survey research to identify the important factors in the ITO relationship	Survey research to identify the success factors in ITO
Data collection methods	Interviews, questionnaires, documents, web information, e-mails		
Data analysis methods	Thematic analysis		

Table 3.2 The number of studied companies and respondents per research study

	Study 1	Study 2	Sum
# of large companies	28[a]	8	37
# of respondents	28[b]	24	52

[a]This number includes also 6 medium-sized companies
[b]This number includes also 6 respondents from medium-sized companies

3.2   Research Process to Achieve the Research Goals

The research process covering each of the three research goals is described below.

3.2.1   Research Process 1 for Achieving Research Goal 1

To achieve research goal 1 (RG1), which is "To develop a method for risk assessment in IT outsourcing", research process 1 has been divided in two steps that are presented below:

1. The first step of the research process 1 is concerning the development of a method for assessing the ITO risks named ITODSM. The research strategy applied for the development of the ITODSM was design science research by using the guidelines of Johannesson and Perjons (2014). The performed main activities to address the research goal 1 have been the followings:

   - Define the requirement for the ITODSM
   - Design and develop the ITODSM
   - Demonstrate the ITODSM
   - Evaluate the ITODSM
   - Communicate knowledge about ITODSM

   To achieve research goal 1 and develop ITODSM we have also identify the risk factors in ITO therefore the development of ITODSM has included a second step that is described below.

2. The second step of the research process 1 is the identification of the risk factors used in the ITODSM and the performed activities using a survey research strategy are shown in Table 3.3.

Table 3.3 Performed activities and how the activities have been performed for the identification of the risk factors in ITO

#	Performed activities	How the activities have been performed
1	Identification of the risk factors in ITO through a research literature review	Research literature review of the risk factors in ITO
2	Analysis of the findings of the literature review and also of the negative consequences of the identified ITO risks from the research literature review	Analysis of the risk factors in ITO
3	Planning and conducting the data collection	Interviews, questionnaires, studied documents and web information about the companies, exchanged e-mails with respondents
4	Analysis of the data collected	Thematic analysis

The results of the performed activities in research process 1 concerning to develop a method for risk assessment in IT outsourcing are presented in Chap. 4, Sect. 4.1.

3.2.2   Research Process 2 for Achieving Research Goal 2

To achieve research goal 2 (RG2), which is "To identify the important factors in IT outsourcing relationship", the performed activities using a survey research strategy are shown in Table 3.4.

The results of the performed activities in research process 2 concerning to identify the important factors in IT outsourcing relationship are presented in Chap. 4, Sect. 4.2.

3.2.3   Research Process 3 for Achieving Research Goal 3

The activities carried out in research process 3 to achieve research goal 3 (RG3), that is "To identify the success factors in IT outsourcing", by using a survey research strategy are shown in Table 3.5.

The results of the performed activities in research process 3 concerning to identify the success factors in IT outsourcing are presented in Chap. 4, Sect. 4.3.

Table 3.4 Performed activities and how the activities have been performed to identify the important factors in IT outsourcing relationship

#	Performed activities	How the activities have been performed
1	Identification of the important factors in the ITO relationship through a research literature review	Research literature review of the important factors in the ITO relationship
2	Analysis of the findings of the literature review and how the important factors that were identified though the research literature review affect the ITO relationship	Analysis of the important factors in the ITO relationship
3	Planning and conducting the data collection	Interviews, questionnaires, studied documents and web information about the companies, exchanged e-mails with respondents
4	Analysis of the data collected	Thematic analysis

Table 3.5 Performed activities and how the activities have been performed to identify the success factors in IT outsourcing

#	Performed activities	How the activities have been performed
1	Identification of the success factors in ITO through a research literature review	Literature review of the success factors in ITO
2	Analysis of the findings of the research literature review and also of the value that the identified success factors from the literature review can create in ITO	Analysis of the success factors in ITO
3	Planning and conducting a survey for data collection	Interviews, questionnaires, studied documents and web information about the companies, exchanged e-mails with respondents
4	Analysis of the data collected	Thematic analysis

References

Bhattacherjee A. (2012). *Social science research: Principles, methods, and practices* (2nd ed.). Creative Commons Attribution-NonCommercial-ShareAlike 3.0. Accessed May 1, 2018, from https://scholarcommons.usf.edu/cgi/viewcontent.cgi?article=1002&context=oa_textbooks

Denscombe, M. (2010). *The good research guide for small-scale social research projects* (4th ed.). Maidenhead: Open University Press.

Hevner, A., March, S., Park, J., & Ram, S. (2004). Design science in information systems research. *MIS Quarterly, 28*(1), 75–105.

Johannesson, P., & Perjons, E. (2014). *An introduction to design science.* Cham: Springer.

Chapter 4
Research Results

Abstract This chapter presents the results covering the three research goals. The results are including the developed method for assessing the risk in ITO, the important relationship factors and success factors in ITO.

Keywords IT outsourcing · Risk assessment · Risk factors · Relationships factors · Success factors · IT decision makers · Method for risk assessment in IT outsourcing

4.1 Results for Research Goal 1: To Develop a Method for Risk Assessment in IT Outsourcing

To achieve the first research goal, a method was developed for assessing the ITO risks, including support for mitigating these risks (ITODSM). This was done in two steps that were presented in Sect. 3.2.1. This method could help both researchers and practitioners in estimating the ITO risks and in this way improve ITO. An application based on the developed method was used to facilitate the testing of this method. The result of RG1 is described below.

4.1.1 The Most Frequent ITO Risk Factors (RFs) in Large Companies

The relevant RFs in ITO are the fundamental factors for assessing the ITO risks. Therefore, these RFs were explored to identify the most frequent ones for use in the development method for risk assessment (ITODSM).

The RFs used in this study originate from Bahli and Rivard (2003), who have reported the most frequent risk factors in ITO. Moreover IT decision makers from different companies were interviewed about their experiences with the RFs that they had most encountered among the ITO RFs described in the ITODSM. The

Table 4.1 The ranking of the most frequent risk factors that cause undesirable outcomes (Hodosi et al. 2013, p. 51)

#	The ranking of the most frequent RFs that cause undesirable outcomes	
	Rivard and Aubert (2008, p. 122)	Findings
1.	Lack of experience and expertise of the supplier with the activity	Specificity of the transaction
2.	Measurement problems	Small number of suppliers
3.	Business uncertainties	Uncertainty with the transaction
4.	Small number of suppliers	Interdependence of activities
5.	Interdependence of activities	Measurement problems

interviews also showed that these respondents have considerable experience with these ITO risk factors and with risk handling in ITO. The results of the study (Hodosi et al. 2013) have showed that the RFs from Bahli and Rivard (2003) are relevant to large companies in Sweden. Regarding the ranking of the RFs' priorities, the results differ regarding the five most frequent RFs that cause undesirable outcomes, as is shown in Table 4.1.

As shown in Table 4.1, the most frequent RFs that cause undesirable outcomes differ regarding their importance. A possible explanation for this deviation could be related to the rapid development of IT and the way in which firms used it. However, the risk factors shown are the most important and frequent ones, and other researchers, like Martens and Teuteberg (2009) and Tho (2011), have also identified the same risk factors in ITO. In this study 17 companies with 18 respondents have confirmed our list of RFs.

4.1.2   The Method for Risk Assessment in IT Outsourcing (ITODSM)

As described above the selection of the frequent risk factors for the ITODSM is a prerequisite for a risk assessment tool. In fact, our research supports the selection and understanding of the risk factors occurring in ITO (Hodosi et al. 2013; Rusu and Hodosi 2011; Andresen et al. 2010; Hodosi and Rusu 2007; Hodosi et al. 2012). For the development of the ITODSM, design science research was used as the research strategy by following the recommendations of Johannesson and Perjons (2014). The ITODSM can support and help IT decision makers in improving their ITO by assessing their ITO risks and using this knowledge to mitigate the ITO risks. Thus, the number of unsuccessful ITOs could be reduced and the research problem could partially be solved.

We have also found that risk exposure (RE) was usefully in the assessment of ITO risks. To calculate it, first the probability of an undesirable outcome together with the loss due to the undesirable outcome has to be estimated. Risk exposure enables the calculation of the probability of loss between the different RFs. Therefore, RE as a measure for assessing the risk in the ITODSM have been used. For example, ITODSM by using RE enables to calculate that, ITO is not recommended if the RE of an individual RF is too high or the sum of all the RFs ($\Sigma_{i=1}^{\infty}(RF_i)$) is too high. Thus, the developed method (the ITODSM) makes possible for the IT decision makers to analyse the current ITO risks and to find the combinations of risk-mitigating actions that result in the lowest total RE (Rusu and Hodosi 2011). However, the ITODSM not only highlights the risks but also suggests ways to mitigate them. For this purpose, a built-in "help" feature was developed in the ITODSM to explain the potential risks with documented cases from ITO research. On the other hand, the number of RFs needs to be limited but still cover all the relevant ITO risks. As mentioned, the ITODSM is based on the RFs from Bahli and Rivard's (2003) framework, to which "ex-ante imperfection" has been added to the scenario "unexpected transition and management costs". The estimation of the probability for each RF brings together experience from the industry, the ITO research literature and TCT. The ITODSM has a scale of four values, and the losses are context-dependent. In cases in which appraisal is not possible, the ITODSM uses the average value of the losses. However, some compromises had to be made, such as when one RF could create several undesirable outcomes. This situation was resolved by pre-setting (increasing) the probability with one level. In other cases, when several RFs produced the same undesirable outcome, it was easier to reach a solution, because the algorithm summarizes the REs for each RF. In the development of the ITODSM, the following components were implemented:

1. Ranking the outcomes from the RE assessment.
2. Assigning severity levels to the risks.
3. Generating suggestions about how the risks could be mitigated.
4. Completing the ITODSM with decision factors that are not risk-based, like transition, in-vestment and service costs and quality assurance assessment.
5. Developing algorithms for the calculation of REs, aggregation of the total RE, estimation of losses and performance of logical choices for risk estimations and handling of various interactions with the users, just to mention a few.

A screenshot showing a menu used in the ITODSM is presented in Fig. 4.1.

The interaction between the ITODSM and the users (IT decision makers) is shown in Fig. 4.1. The ITODSM asks the user: "Is your core business dependent on your outsourcing object" and displays four alternatives. The user highlights

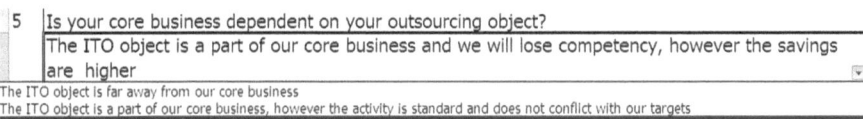

Fig. 4.1 A screenshot showing a menu in the ITODSM together with the alternative answers

Summary of the evaluation result:

Total Risk Exposure:	10,29
Average Risk Exposure Is:	0,2
Highest Risk Exposure is:	0,86
Lowest Risk Exposure is:	0,02
Number of Risk Exposures > 0.2	19
Number of Critical Risk Exposures, >0.4	6
Standard Dev. (%):	20,35
Recommendation:	Start with fixing your critical issues, then you can start thinking about outsourcing!

Fig. 4.2 A snapshot showing a summary of the assessment results generated by the ITODSM

option 3, which is, "The ITO object is a part of our core ...". Additionally, for each question help can be achieved to guide the users.

The results obtained using the ITODSM are shown in Fig. 4.2.

Figure 4.2 shows the result of an example of the ITO risk assessment. This result includes the following information:

1. The total RE, which is the aggregated RE and is the value that should be compared with the decision makers' risk aversion;
2. The average of the RE, which gives a figure about the general RE level;
3. The highest RE, which is the most critical item for the ITO decision;
4. The lowest RE, which is the least critical item for the ITO decision;
5. The number of REs $< = 0.2$; in this case there are 19 questions that do not receive recommendations to mitigate the risks;
6. The number of critical REs $= > 0.4$; in this case there are 6 questions for which the risk exposure is higher and outsourcing the IT is not recommended;
7. The standard deviation of the RE, which describes the dispersion of the different risk exposures;
8. The recommendation given to the user. In this case it is highly recommended to undertake risk mitigation before ITO.

Moreover, the ITODSM presents a final recommendation, and, if ITO is in the planning stage, the decision maker is advised whether to outsource IT or not. For those who have already outsourced their IT, the ITODSM advises how to improve their ITO by mitigating the ITO risks. The evaluation of the ITODSM as part of the artefact design was performed in two steps, first by two CIOs. We have implemented the received feedback and then four other IT decision makers have tested the updated ITODSM.

The ITODSM was evaluated by IT decision makers from two large companies in Sweden with 20 years of experience of in- and outsourcing. A short description of the companies' IT is shown below (Hodosi and Rusu 2013, p. 26):

> Both companies have a centralized IT with all corporate databases and enterprise systems placed in two European sites. A network connects all locations with data and voice. Application development of the core business software is separated from the IT unit. The outsourced IT is divided into applications and IT infrastructure hardware, with different suppliers. The coordination between the two areas is coordinated by the suppliers. There is a mixture of IT infrastructure, with client-server and large mainframes and old legacy systems, along with the newest research and development tools, large national adaptations, and an always-increasing budget for the IT. Both MNCs regularly measure the users' (employees') satisfaction with IT. Both companies participate in different third-party benchmarking areas and belong to the mature organizations in Europe.

The two IT decision makers contributed to the improvement of the ITODSM. The respondents from these companies acknowledged that the risk factors in ITO are essential, that a systematic process to handle them is a good idea and that the ITODSM facilitates this process. The IT decision-makers knew the RFs of the ITODSM, and they had tried to mitigate these ITO risks or had succeeded in eliminating the negative consequences. The positive feedback and suggestions for improvements indicated that the practitioners saw the need for the ITODSM to assess the ITO risks and help them to improve their ITO.

In the following section, we describe how IT decision makers from large companies have accepted ITODSM.

4.1.3   Acceptance of the ITODSM

Even if the ITODSM works satisfactorily, why should a manager accept it when, over a long period, many decisions on IT outsourcing have been taken successfully following established practice without such tools? The answer to this question is that there is still a need to develop a method that facilitates complex ITO decisions. The method has to have the functionality that ITO decision makers are missing, and the degree to which the method is acceptable for them should also be determined. We studied the acceptance of the ITODSM along with how the method can be improved to achieve even better acceptance levels. The won knowledge and result we published in Andresen et al. (2010). We used the technology acceptance model (TAM[1]) in four companies to investigate the users' acceptance of the ITODSM. The respondents from the buyer organisations had the job positions: executive, CIO, Head of procurement and sales manager and all of them had several years of experience with

---

[1]TAM (Davis 1989) is a theory in IT which describe a model of how people will accept and use a new technology. Some factors affect their decision about how and when they will use it.

ITO. The companies belong to the large ones in Sweden representing advisory services, production and Research and Development.

After presenting the ITODSM, the participants could use the ITODSM. Then, when they felt confident with the tool, the data collection started. Here we show some shortened comments from the interviews: (1) "We are using risk evaluation, but not in this deep level like RFs", (2) "This must be the new way of analysing ITO", (3) "Comparing risks is easy and becomes more objective", (4) "For each case, there is an advice", (4) "ITODSM, does not need Internet and my secret data is on my laptop" and (5) "Every step is documented and includes examples I can use in our steering group".

We used thematic analysis for the data analysis. The identified most important themes were (1) usability, (2) suitability, (3) effectiveness and (4) satisfaction. Apart from this analysis, it was found that firstly, to accept a decision method in ITO, trust must exist; that is, the ITODSM has to deliver reliable results and cover those risk factors that the ITO decision makers have encountered or for which there is the potential to arise. However, as noticed, none of the respondents pointed out an ITO risk factor that was missing. This can be seen as a positive result, so it is possible to say that the ITODSM could address the current ITO problems caused by the implemented ITO risk factors. In fact, the completeness was validated. Indirectly, the functional requirements regarding risk coverage and assessment were also evaluated.

The result of the evaluation was positive acceptance by the IT decision makers in three out of the four companies. Apart from the acceptance of the method, several additional features were suggested by some of the IT decision makers from these four companies. Most of these, however, are beyond the scope of this research and are more suitable for market-driven software, such as checking suppliers' financial stability (a procurement problem). Some suggestions were contradictory; for example, one company wanted the number of questions to be reduced, while another wanted to add more questions. It was concluded that the ITODSM was generally acceptable "as it was". In summary, the interviews also confirmed that the RFs implemented in the method were the ones that the IT decision makers have encountered in their IT outsourcing, and they appreciated the guidelines provided by the ITODSM about how to mitigate the risks.

We also observed that all the respondents were able to use the ITODSM with a short introduction. This was not surprising; the first two CIOs used the ITODSM without an introduction. This indicates that the usability of the ITODSM is acceptable. In fact, one of the companies' respondents clearly stated that all the help needed is documented in the ITODSM. Furthermore, all the respondents agreed that the ITODSM enabled them to assess the ITO risks and in this way improve their ITO or guided them on whether to outsource IT or not. Moreover, an observation was made by one of the companies' respondents that an additional way of using the ITODSM would be in communication with various stakeholders to create joint work and discuss the ITO risks. This indicates that the implemented documentation in the ITODSM is useful.

4.2   Results for Research Goal 2: To Identify the Important Factors in IT Outsourcing Relationships

A good relationship between the IT service provider and the buyer is an enabler of successful IT outsourcing. The goal of the study was to consider the most important factors that can create a good ITO relationship between the ITO provider and the service buyer. The focus of our research is the service buyer, but the providers for four of the buying organization were also interviewed to understand both parties' ITO targets.

The respondents from the buyer organisations had the job positions: project executive, IT manager, contract manager, head of outsourcing, IT program manager, CIO/Vice President, sourcing manager and all of these respondents had several years of experience with ITO. The broad coverage of the industries in this study gives a good overview of ITO relationship in the organizations in Sweden.

The data collected from the respondents was analysed using thematic analysis with the NVivo 11, a qualitative analyses software. The identified most important themes were (1) conflict and conflict resolution, (2) culture, (3) communication and (4) trust. Apart from this analysis, it was found that expectation management has been a key issue. To improve it, it is necessary with better requirement specifications and contract management. However, as noticed, none of the respondents pointed out a missing ITO relationship factor. This can be seen as a positive result, so it is possible to say that our list of the important ITO relationship factor has full coverage. In fact, the completeness was validated.

We have explored the ITO relationships, identified the important factors for successful IT outsourcing and ranked them according to their importance. The result has been published in the research paper Hodosi et al. (2012). The main important factors in ITO relationships are presented below.

1. Contract management
   It can be considered that contract management is a main factor for ITO success. This is what Williamson also observed when formulating TCT (Williamson 1985). A good ITO relationship helps the work with contract management. Vice versa, a bad contract leads to a bad relationship.
2. Expectation management
   The study points out the importance of examining this factor for successful ITO. If the service buyer does not receive what is expected, then the relationship is impaired and the ITO will not be successful. The challenge is to formulate unambiguous requirement specifications in the contract.
3. Communication
   This is the most important ITO relationship factor. ITO communication has to take place at all working levels, both planned and ad hoc, and this could be facilitated by communication tools.
4. Conflict and conflict resolution
   Conflicts are unavoidable in such a complex environment. A well-working conflict resolution system is therefore necessary. The study showed that these factors are a general problem and ranked them as the second most important factors.

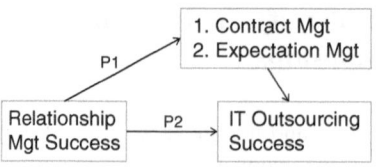

Relationship Factors that support the IT Outsourcing success:
1. Communication
2. Conflict & Conflict Resolution
3. Trust, Commitment and Cooperation

Fig. 4.3 How IT outsourcing success is influenced by relationship management, contract management and expectation management together with the relationships factors that support the IT outsourcing success (Hodosi et al. 2012, p. 8)

5. Trust, commitment and cooperation

These three interrelated factors are the third most important ones for a successful ITO relationship. The respondents understood them.

The study also verified the following statements:

1. Successful management of the ITO relationship positively influences contract management.
2. Successful management of the ITO relationship positively influences the success of IT outsourcing.

A critical review of the results shows that some factors differ from the expected ones. This study found that behavioural factors, like trust, commitment and cooperation, are not at the top of the list of priorities. It could be considered that the interviewees represent relatively large ITO with many sites that run applications with high asset specificity and no stops are tolerated. Trust and commitment are reinforced with specific contract commitment and cooperation and are an integral part of the service delivery. Some support for this study can be found in the research by Kern and Willcocks (2002) and Perrin and Pervan (2005).

Figure 4.3 shows the two results of this study. On the left side, it is shown that a successful relationship facilitates the contract management and expectation management, but also a successful IT outsourcing. On the right side, the relationship factors, in prioritized order with three levels are shown.

In a study performed by Cullen et al. (2017), for investigating contracts and ITO relationships, the researchers have recommended on placing the efforts on improving the ITO relationship instead of contracting techniques. As we noticed, their focus was on behavioural approaches. Moreover, they also observed the importance of conflict resolution, in all working and management levels.

4.3   Results of Research Goal 3: To Identify the Success Factors in IT Outsourcing

The success factors (SFs) in IT outsourcing are not well represented in the research literature (Hodosi and Rusu 2008, p. 3). On the other hand, the research literature is available in abundance about providers, but the research focus is on their own business, which is not necessarily the same as the service buyers' companies.[2]

The research in this book concerning research goal 3 identified a list of 11 SFs, reduced from an initial 88 SFs by eliminating duplicates and excluding SFs that are not specific to ITO or not useful for service buyer companies. The last two criteria need some clarification. An SF that is not ITO specific is, for example, a lack of knowledge of leadership. As in many disciplines, leadership is necessary to guide and organize the employees; ITO is no different, and therefore this SF is not ITO specific. The last criterion, not being usefully for the service buyer companies, refers to those proposed SFs for which the value that they could create for the buying organization is not known. For example, a proposed SF that is not useful for the service buyer company is good for the service provider. The study also observed that not all the SFs related to service buyers found in the research literature are necessarily useful for them. In the case of "risk sharing," for instance, in the worst case, the provider can suffer payment losses for not delivering the contracted service, while the buyer, on the other hand, stands to lose customer confidence and in worst case loose customers, and consequently, their survival is jeopardized. How can these outcomes be divided equally? All the respondents verified that they took risks and did not consider them as SFs. "Win/win" provides another example: the target for the service buyer is to have an acceptable contract, covering the needs within the cost as cheaply as possible, but within the cost limit. How the provider resolves the cost coverage is not the buyer's task, and it is not visible for the service buyer, like costs and efforts. How can this work in practice? None of the respondents found this item to be useful. In summary, the main findings of this research study are the following:

1. The value that each SF could create for the service buyer company.
2. The risk mitigation that each of the SFs could provide to improve ITO.
3. The importance of prioritizing the SFs for the implementation.

The stage in the ITO life cycle during which the SFs should be implemented.

Based on the survey among the respondents, a prioritized list of the SFs was created and it is presented in Table 4.2.

Table 4.2 shows the identified SFs, ranked on four priority levels. The recommendation for ITO decision makers on how to implement these SFs is first to implement the SFs on priority level one, then to work on those SFs on level two and so on. In each of these four groups, the SFs have equal importance. Based on the "eight-phase life cycle" of Cullen and Willcocks (2003), the study also provided recommendations regarding when in the ITO life cycle each SF should be implemented along with the value. These recommendations will further help ITO decision makers to plan the implementation of the SFs in ITO.

---

[2]The differences in targets are the "buyer/seller dilemma"; as, "for example, the service provider wants a long contract, whilst the service buyer a shorter one to be able to swap and select the best provider in the market. Another example is that the service provider wishes a high price and the buyer a low price" (Hodosi and Rusu (2013), p. 19).

Table 4.2 The prioritized list of the success factors in ITO according to their importance (Hodosi and Rusu 2013, p. 28)

#	Success factors (SFs)	Priority level
1.	Outsource only when it makes good business sense	1
2.	Have a detailed plan including all the resources, competencies and costs for the next several years before signing the contract	
3.	Determine what to outsource and what to keep inside the organization	2
4.	Measure the contract fulfilment	
5.	Maintain good communication between the organizations	
6.	Select a supplier that fits your business culture and size	
7.	Use flexible contracts and update them regularly	3
8.	Prepare the personnel of the outsourcing company for their new role	
9.	Make sure that the provider uses the standard tools and processes defined as part of the operational model	
10.	Do not outsource broken processes; improve them first	
11.	The outsourcer should undertake due diligence to understand, quantify and qualify its outsourcing needs before starting the request for information	4

The highest priority is 1. The items with the same priority level are not ranked further within that priority group

The data collection is based on 12 large companies with 25 respondents. The interviewee's' job positions were 13 CIOs, 4, IT service managers, 3 sourcing managers, only to mention some of the most frequent ones. All of them have several years of experience with IT and ITO. The 12 large companies cover the largest companies in Sweden, all of them are multinational and most of their revenues and operations are from outside Sweden. The broad coverage of the industries in this study gives a good overview of how success factors are understood and handled by the organizations in Sweden.

References

Andresen, C., Hodosi, G., Saprykina, I., & Rusu, L. (2010). User acceptance of a software tool for decision making in IT outsourcing: A qualitative study in large companies from Sweden. In M. Lytras, P. Ordonez De Pablos, A. Ziderman, A. Roulstone, H. Maurer, & J. Imber (Eds.), *Knowledge management, information systems, e-learning, and sustainability*. Communications in computer and information science (Vol. 111, pp. 277–288). Berlin: Springer-Verlag.

Bahli, B., & Rivard, S. (2003). A validation of measures associated with the risk factors in information technology outsourcing. In *Proceedings of the 36th Hawaii International Conference on System Sciences (HICSS'03)*. Island of Hawaii: IEEE Computer Society.

Cullen, S., & Willcocks, L. (2003). *Intelligent IT outsourcing eight building blocks to success*. New York: Elsevier Butterworth-Heinemann.

Cullen, S., Shanks, G., Davern, M., & Willcocks, L. (2017). A framework for relationships in outsourcing: Contract management archetypes. In *Proceedings of the 50th Hawaii International Conference on System Sciences*. https://doi.org/10.24251/HICSS.2017.652.

Davis, F. (1989). Perceived usefulness, perceived ease of use and user acceptance of information technology. *MIS Quarterly, 13*(3), 319–340.

Hodosi, G., & Rusu, L. (2007). A software tool that supports decision for companies to outsource information technology or not. In *MCIS 2007 Proceedings 1, 2007 Mediterranean Conference on Information Systems*, Paper 22, San Servolo, Venice, Italy: Association for Information Systems.

Hodosi, G., & Rusu, L. (2008). Information technology outsourcing: A case study of best practices in two Swedish global companies. In *Proceedings of the Mediterranean Conference on Information Systems (MCIS 2008)*, Paper 7, Hammamet, Tunisia: Association for Information Systems.

Hodosi, G., & Rusu, L. (2013). How do critical success factors contribute to a successful IT outsourcing: A study of large multinational companies. *Journal of Information Technology Theory and Application (JITTA), 14*(1), 17–43.

Hodosi, G., Rusu, L., & Seungho, C. (2012). A risk based view of influential factors in IT outsourcing relationship for large multinational companies: A service buyer perspective. *International Journal of Social and Organizational Dynamics in IT, 2*(3), 29–47.

Hodosi, G., Manavi, S., & Rusu, L. (2013). Risk factors in IT outsourcing and the theories decision makers use to resolve them. *International Journal of Social and Organizational Dynamics in IT (IJSODIT), 3*(2), 41–54.

Johannesson, P., & Perjons, E. (2014). *An introduction to design science*. Cham: Springer.

Kern, T., & Willcocks, L. (2002). Exploring relationships in information technology outsourcing: The interaction approach. *European Journal of Information Systems, 11*, 3–19.

Martens, B., & Teuteberg, F. (2009). Why management matters in IT outsourcing – A systematic literature review and elements of a research agenda. In P. Newell et al. (Ed.), *Information systems in a globalising world: Challenges, ethics, and practices*. Proceedings of 17th European Conference on Information Systems, Paper 451, Verona, Italy: Association for Information Systems.

Perrin, B., & Pervan, G. (2005). IT outsourcing relationship management and performance measurement system effectiveness. In *16th Australasian Conference on Information Systems IT Outsourcing* (pp. 1–10). Sydney: Association for Information Systems.

Rivard, S., & Aubert, B. (Eds.). (2008). *Information technology outsourcing*. Advanced in management information systems (Vol. 8, pp. 25–35).

Rusu, L., & Hodosi, G. (2011). Assessing the risk exposure in IT outsourcing for large companies. *International Journal of Information Technology and Management, 10*(1), 24–44.

Tho, J. (2011). *Managing the risks of IT outsourcing*. New York: Routledge.

Williamson, O. (1985). *The economic institutions of capitalism – Firms, markets, relational contracting*. London: The Free Press.

Chapter 5
Contributions, Limitations and Further Research

Abstract This chapter presents the contributions, limitations of this research and recommendations for future research.

Keywords IT outsourcing · Risk assessment · Risk factors · Relationships factors · Success factors

5.1 Overview of the Contributions

IT outsourcing is today a frequently used strategy in many large companies for different purposes, for example to focus more on the core business or on buying state-of-the-art technology. Companies world-wide invest a large amount of money to achieve a successful IT outsourcing. However, in several cases they fail to achieve either cost savings or the agreed service quality or both.

The results of the research presented in this book can support researchers in developing new methods for assessing the ITO risks, in increasing the understanding of the most important ITO relationship factors and in identifying new ITO success factors in large companies. As was described in Chap. 3, the data collection was conducted in two studies, Study 1 performed between 2007 and 2014 and Study 2, between 2015 until February 2016. But, the results in Study 2, has not shown any differences concerning the identified risk factors, important relationship factors and ITO success factors found in Study 1.

This research also provides some practical implications for IT decision makers by offering insights into how to improve ITO by evaluating the risks and proposing how to mitigate them, identify important factors that could improve ITO relationship, and identify ITO success factors along with the stage in the ITO life cycle during which to implement them to create value. The main contributions cover the raised research goals and are shown in Table 5.1.

A detailed description of the main contributions of this research is presented below.

Table 5.1 The research goals and the main contributions of this research

Research goals	Main contributions
RG1: To develop a method for risk assessment in IT outsourcing	A method for assessing the risks in ITO
RG2: To identify the important factors in IT outsourcing relationships	A prioritized list of the important ITO relationship factors that could improve the ITO relationship
RG3: To identify the success factors in IT outsourcing	A prioritized list of ITO success factors for large companies and when to implement them in the ITO life cycle to create value

5.1.1   The Main Contribution to Research Goal 1

The main contribution to research goal 1 is the development of a method for risk assessment in ITO (ITODSM) that can support both researchers in developing other ITO risk evaluation methods based on risk exposure and also IT decision makers in improving their ITO. The new method can consider new risks in ITO, in this way improving the assessment of the risks and providing better support for IT decision makers. This knowledge could also encourage researchers to develop other ITO risk assessment methods and in this way support practitioners in assessing complex ITO, which could lead to better decision making. Moreover, the ITODSM has practical implications for IT outsourcing decision makers, because this method is a neutral one[1] and its value was confirmed by most of the respondents.

To achieve the research goal 1 we have also identified the ITO risks by reviewing the research literature on ITO. As was mentioned above, the risks factors (RFs) are fundamental to ITODSM. Therefore, a study of the RFs was necessary to attain research goal 1 and identify these RFs and also how they affect large companies in Sweden. The results have shown that the transaction cost theory covers all the ITO risk factors completely and agency theory has entirely not covered two RFs and has partially covered four RFs. Concerning the core competency theory, the research study shows that only one RF is thoroughly covered and partially there are two RFs covered (Hodosi et al. 2013).

In summary, the RFs we have identified in achieving the research goal 1 can help ITO researchers to understand how these theories cover these ITO risk factors. Additionally, we have presented the differences between those RFs recommended by Bahli and Rivard (2003) and this research's result regarding the most frequent

---

[1]To outsource or not is for the ITODSM neutral, what for a contracted advisor of ITO, who might have the interest to be involved in a planned ITO, might not be unbiased. The developed tool is conservative; if the created value by outsourcing IT is low, the given advice will be to minimize the risks, in this case, not to outsource. This view is based on the transaction cost theory (Williamson 1985), if possible, risks should be avoided.

RFs in ITO and help those who are researching risk mitigation and plan to reduce the adverse effects of their current ITO risks.

5.1.2   The Main Contribution to Research Goal 2

The main contributions to research goal 2 are the identification of the main important ITO relationship factors and the development of a prioritized list of ITO relationship factors based on the buyers' requirements for successful ITO, which was verified with providers. This list could help researchers in this field to focus relationship studies on the direction of contracting. This knowledge confirms Williamson's (1985) findings concerning that contracting is the most problematic challenge in any outsourcing. For ITO decision makers, the developed list could help to improve the relationships with their providers by implementing the highest prioritized relationship factors.[2]

The research also has verified the following two propositions: (1) successful management of the ITO relationship positively influences contract management and that (2) successful management of the ITO relationship positively influences IT outsourcing. In this way these findings can provide researchers and IT decision makers usefully information about potential improvements in the field of contracting and ITO relationships.

5.1.3   The Main Contribution to Research Goal 3

The main contributions to research goal 3 are the identification of the ITO success factors (SFs) in large companies and the development of a prioritized list of the SFs in ITO according to their importance together with the value that they could create when implemented in the ITO life cycle. Therefore, IT practitioners could use these SFs in ITO to improve their IT outsourcing by deciding when in the ITO lifecycle to implement the SFs and create value.

Apart from the identified SFs in ITO in large companies, it was investigated whether these SFs in ITO could be applied to medium-sized companies. The study has found that the SFs are the same but that there are differences in their priority ranking (according to their importance) that could indicate to researchers in ITO that "company size matters".

---

[2]In a study published in 2017 and entitled "Review of 23 Years of Empirical Research on Information Technology Outsourcing Decisions and Outcomes", that is including 1170 empirical examinations, Lacity et al. (2017) presents most of the ITO relationship important factors that we have also identified in our research.

5.2 Limitations and Further Research

The following significant limitations should be taken into account for interpreting the results of this research study. In this research, the focus of the investigations was on large companies in Sweden and it is supposed that these results could be used in the Nordic countries and probably other countries as well. The literature review we have performed has indicated similarities between the companies in Sweden and those in Europe, North America and Australia. But a comparative study would be necessary to identify the differences.

Another limitation is that small companies were not studied; only a comparison of the success factors between large and medium-sized companies was made to gain a better understanding of how differences in size affect IT outsourcing. The result is indicative. Therefore, further research is needed. The data collected in this research is qualitative, and additional data from a quantitative approach could increase the significance of the results.

The research in this book has explored only IT services; therefore, software development was not included in this study. Minor adaptations and configurations are however part of the regular IT service delivery.

The information about the studied companies has not been presented to ensure confidentiality. Moreover, almost all of the respondents have wished to remain anonymous. Furthermore, the responsibility for this ethical consideration, namely to ensure anonymity, was taken in consideration in several different ways. Firstly, by reporting the number of employees, most of the larger companies in Sweden could easily be identified. Therefore, the real numbers of companies' employees presented in our research were not mentioned exactly. Secondly, the precise working area of the companies was not given to avoid companies being recognized. Last but not least, the respondents' positions were "standardized" and company-specific positions were not mentioned. But all these limitations have no impact on the achievement of the research goals and are clearly mentioned to explain why the results are presented in this way.

The research presented in this book contributes to the improvement of ITO, in different ways like a method for ITO risk assessment and risk mitigation, a prioritized list of the main important factors for improving ITO relationships and how to implement the most effective success factors in the ITO life cycle. A future study could explore how all these implemented improvements of ITO can reach the targeted results in other types of companies, for example, public organizations. The risk factors in ITO explored in our research are based on transaction cost theory, agency theory and core competence theory, and in a future research other theories could be examined to increase the knowledge in this research field.

IT outsourcing is a strategic tool for creating a competitive advantage that can also encourage innovations in all aspects in which IT services are involved. Innovation in ITO is a process that has to be planned, negotiated and consequently improved. A good ITO relationship enables this work, but research in this area was not included, although it is highly recommended to be explored in a further research.

This research has intended to achieve the main research goal to improve ITO by focusing on risks, relationships and success factors in ITO. The results obtained do not exclude other ways of resolving the research problem and improve ITO. Further studies could select other research directions for improving ITO like, e.g., the study of the influences of contract management (Hodosi et al. 2012; Williamson 1985), organizational culture (Aasi et al. 2015) and tacit knowledge (Hodosi et al. 2017) on ITO, just to mention a few of them.

References

Aasi, P., Nunes, I., Rusu, L., & Hodosi, G. (2015). Does organizational culture matter in IT outsourcing relationships? In *Proceedings of the 48th Annual Hawaii International Conference on System Sciences (HICSS-48)* (pp. 4691–4699). Kauai, HI: IEEE Computer Society.

Bahli, B., & Rivard, S. A. (2003). Validation of measures associated with the risk factors in information technology outsourcing. In *Proceedings of the 36th Hawaii International Conference on System Sciences (HICSS'03)*. Hilton Waikoloa Village, HI: IEEE Computer Society.

Hodosi, G., Rusu, L., & Seungho, C. (2012). A risk based view of influential factors in IT outsourcing relationship for large multinational companies: A service buyer perspective. *International Journal of Social and Organizational Dynamics in IT, 2*(3), 29–47.

Hodosi, G., Manavi, S., & Rusu, L. (2013). Risk factors in IT outsourcing and the theories decision makers use to resolve them. *International Journal of Social and Organizational Dynamics in IT (IJSODIT), 3*(2), 41–54.

Hodosi, G., Johansson, D., & Rusu, L. (2017). Does it matter the loss of tacit knowledge in IT outsourcing? A study in a Swedish governmental agency. *Procedia Computer Science, 121*, 491–502.

Lacity, M., Yan, A., & Khan, S. (2017). Review of 23 years of empirical research on information technology outsourcing decisions and outcomes. In *Proceedings of the 50th Hawaii International Conference on System Sciences* (pp. 5214–5224). Waikoloa, HI: IEEE Computer Society.

Williamson, O. (1985). *The economic institutions of capitalism – Firms, markets, relational contracting*. London: The Free Press.